D0194815

Disney · PIXAR
INSIDE OUT

The
EMOTIONS'
SURVIVAL · GUIDE

Special thanks to Dr. Vicki Zakrzewski,
Education Director, Greater Good Science Center
at the University of California, Berkeley

Disney · PIXAR
INSIDE OUT

The
EMOTIONS'
SURVIVAL · GUIDE

by Joy, Sadness, Disgust, Fear, and Anger

Random House New York

INTRODUCTION

Hello, and welcome to the Emotions' Survival Guide! We're so happy you're here!

Joy

She's happy. I'm just here.

Sadness

There you go again, Sadness. Trying to scare everyone away before they even get to the first page.

Disgust

What you should really be scared of is turning the page! You could get a paper cut, a hangnail, or a headache from reading too closely!

Fear

I'll tell you what gives *me* a headache—listening to you people all day! Turn the page to put me out of my misery. . . .

Anger

CONTENTS

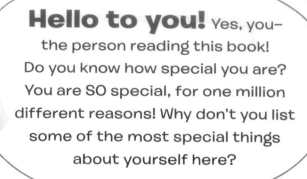

Hello to you! Yes, you—
the person reading this book!
Do you know how special you are?
You are SO special, for one million
different reasons! Why don't you list
some of the most special things
about yourself here?

1. ....
....

2. ....
....

3. ....
....

4. ....
....

5. ....
....

All About Me

Paste a photo of yourself here!

Name: ....

Age: .... **Birthday:** ....

Hometown: ....

Fun Facts About Me: ....

....

....

....

....

....

Joy

Hello again! My name is **Joy**, and I'm one of Riley's Emotions. Riley is my girl, and I try to keep her as happy as I can. What makes you happy? Making lists makes me happy!

THINGS THAT MAKE JOY HAPPY

- Ice Hockey
- Sunshine
- Summer
- Puppies
- Freshly Baked Cookies
- Ice Cream

THINGS THAT MAKE ME HAPPY

1. ....

....

2. ....

....

3. ....

....

4. ....

....

5. ....

....

6. ....

....

7. ....

....

8. ....

....

Sadness

Oh, is it my turn now?
Okay, well, here goes.
I'm **Sadness**. I'm one of
Riley's Emotions, too, just like Joy . . .
except I'm nothing like Joy at all. I focus
on doom and gloom, like when Riley had to
move away from her old life and friends.
That was the worst. When I'm sad,
I sometimes lie on the floor and cry
and cry and cry. . . .

Wow, that's a whole lot of
sadness, Sadness! How about
we focus on some ways to
cheer up when we feel sad?

Yeah, okay.

Here's another list!

WHAT TO DO WHEN YOU'RE SAD

- Draw a picture.

- List ten things that make you happy.

- Talk about what's going on with someone you trust.

- Read a book that will make you laugh.

- Listen to music that makes you want to dance.

- Go for a walk.

- Exercise!

- Help another person or a pet.

- Write about three people you're grateful for and why.

- Remember that you'll feel better with time!

Anger

All right, enough sad stuff! I'm **Anger**, and it's my turn. I'll tell you what makes me angry—everything! Healthy pizza! No dessert! Getting sent to bed early!

HERE ARE SOME OF MY FAVORITE THINGS TO SAY

- Get out of my way!
- It's not fair!
- I want it now!

Ways to calm down

- Take some deep breaths.

- Count to ten really slowly.

- Go for a walk or run.

- Yell something silly like "Peanut butter sandwiches!"

- Think of a peaceful place.

The first step toward resolving anger is to calm down!

How to solve the problem

- Ask yourself, "What do I want in this situation?"

- Consider other people's feelings.

- Create a solution together!

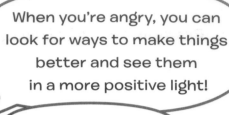

When you're angry, you can look for ways to make things better and see them in a more positive light!

Oh yeah? Give me **ONE** example.

How about three?

Example #1: You get a bad grade on a test.

 I hate this class!

 I'll study harder next time!

Example #2: You didn't make the hockey team.

 It's a stupid team anyway!

 I'll find a different way to get involved!

Example #3: You stubbed your toe.

 I'll break whatever stubbed my toe!

 Stubbing your toe can be fun!

 That doesn't even make sense.

 Okay, that last one is a bad example. But the point is, it's best to calm down when you're angry so you can come up with a solution to the problem.

Now it's your turn! Write down some challenges you're facing, and the right and wrong way to handle each situation.

Challenge #1: ....

....

✗ Wrong ....

....

✓ Right ....

....

Challenge #2: ....

....

✗ Wrong ....

....

✓ Right ....

....

Challenge #3: ....

....

✗ Wrong ....

....

✓ Right ....

....

Challenge #4: ....

....

✗ Wrong ....

....

✓ Right ....

....

DANGER
KEEP OUT!

Fear

There are so many things to be scared of in this world. That's where I come in. I'm **Fear**, and I'm scared of everything!

FEAR'S FAVORITE THINGS TO BE SCARED OF

- Darkness
- Heights (and falling from them!)
- Bugs
- Giving a speech in class
- Snakes
- Nightmares
- Tests and pop quizzes
- Bad report cards
- Bullies
- Having a nightmare about falling from a great height in the dark while giving a speech in class about bugs and snakes!

HOW TO OVERCOME YOUR FEAR

- Take a deep breath.

- Say to yourself, "I can do this."

- Talk to an adult about your fear.

- Name your fear out loud.
(This can make it less scary!)

- Take small steps to face your fear.

- Write down the worst thing
that can happen.

- Write down what is most likely to happen!

Disgust

I have to go last? REALLY? That's so typical. I'm **Disgust**, another one of Riley's Emotions. I'm here to tell you everything you need to know to be cool and popular—like me—and not deal with anything gross. And there's plenty out there that's gross: broccoli, rats, garbage . . . the list goes on.

Create a list of things that are gross. Now think of things that are even *more* disgusting than the ones you just wrote down. That will make your first list look a lot better!

A Little Gross

1. ....
2. ....
3. ....
4. ....
5. ....

REALLY, REALLY GROSS

1. ....
2. ....
3. ....
4. ....
5. ....

Family

Riley's family has an important place in her heart. That's why family makes up one of her core Islands of Personality. Everyone's family is different and special in its own way!

WHO ARE THE PEOPLE IN YOUR FAMILY?

....

....

....

....

....

....

Paste a photo of you
and your family here!

Parents

Part of growing up is learning how to handle your parents. Sometimes parents say and do things that are really embarrassing, like painting their faces and cheering loudly in an arena packed with people.

Or calling you a silly nickname— *in front of your friends!*

That's when it helps to remember that they're only doing these things because they love you and want to show you they care!

Here are some ways to show your parents that you care about them, too.

- Tell them what's going on in your life.

- Let them know where you are at all times.

- Study hard in school.

- Help out around the house.

- Answer the phone when they call you.

- Spend time with them.

- Listen to their stories and advice.

Friends

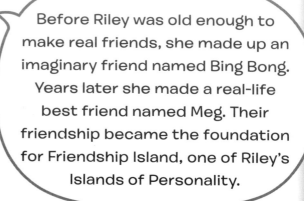

Before Riley was old enough to make real friends, she made up an imaginary friend named Bing Bong. Years later she made a real-life best friend named Meg. Their friendship became the foundation for Friendship Island, one of Riley's Islands of Personality.

WHO ARE YOUR BEST FRIENDS?

....

....

....

....

....

....

Paste a photo of you and
your friends here!

Here are some fun ways to make memories with your friends!

- Have a sleepover.
- Play video or board games.
- Create a time capsule!
- Plant a garden.
- Make up your own language!
- Create a secret handshake.
- Play mini golf or shoot some hoops.

WHAT ARE SOME OTHER FUN THINGS YOU CAN DO WITH A FRIEND?

1. ....
....

2. ....
....

3. ....
....

4. ....
....

5. ....
....

Crushes

One of the things in Riley's mind is an Imaginary Boyfriend Generator! It's fun to have crushes, and normal to want to be liked by the person you like. But it's also important to find balance and not worry too much about what someone thinks of you.

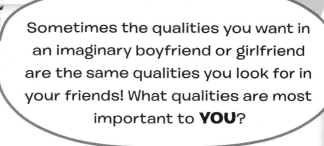

Sometimes the qualities you want in an imaginary boyfriend or girlfriend are the same qualities you look for in your friends! What qualities are most important to **YOU**?

CHEERFUL SMART

FUNNY RESPECTFUL

CREATIVE BRAVE

TRUSTWORTHY FRIENDLY

ATHLETIC TALENTED

KIND CLEVER

GENEROUS

CARING

HONEST

ADVENTUROUS

Remember that one day, the right person will like you just for being yourself. Until then, focus on becoming the best person you can be!

Silly Stuff

Goofball Island is another of Riley's Islands of Personality. It focuses on the importance of being silly. Being silly is a good way to keep life fun and not take things too seriously!

Here are some fun ways to keep yourself laughing!

- Watch a comedy movie with your friends.
- Read a funny book!
- Look at pictures or watch videos of animals doing silly things.
- Ask your family to tell you stories or show you pictures from when you were little.
- Sing karaoke, or make your own music video!

Setting Goals

Hockey Island is another one of Riley's Islands of Personality. Riley loves playing hockey! What kinds of things do you like to do? It's important to pursue hobbies that make you happy and give you new goals to aim for!

WHAT ARE SOME GOALS YOU HOPE TO ACHIEVE THIS YEAR?

1. ....

....

2. ....

....

3. ....

....

4. ....

....

5. ....

....

6. ....

....

7. ....

....

Hobbies

What new things would you like to try or learn more about? **Circle them!**

Ballet

Gardening

Sewing

Astronomy

Cooking

Photography

Knitting

Collecting

Bird-watching

Geology

Painting

Running

Baking

Model-building

Chess

Volunteering

Martial arts

Beadwork

Reading

Yoga

Origami

Basketball	Dance
Singing	Fencing
Soapmaking	**Genealogy**
Scrapbooking	**Camping**
Computer coding	Darts
Languages	Bowling
Jumping rope	**Jigsaw puzzles**
Woodworking	**Old movies**
Magic tricks	Guitar
Pottery	**Architecture**
Crossword puzzles	Cake decorating
Bicycling	**Drawing**
Calligraphy	**Wrestling**
Baseball	Acting
Juggling	**Tennis**
Horseback riding	Swimming

Making Memories

The Memory Dump is where all of Riley's memories go when she doesn't need them anymore.

Like Riley, you have thousands of memories. Some are good, some are bad, some are neither—and some are both! Memories can change over time. Something that once embarrassed you (like falling into a mud puddle) might make you laugh one day!

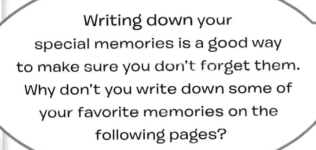

Writing down your special memories is a good way to make sure you don't forget them. Why don't you write down some of your favorite memories on the following pages?

Here are some suggestions to help you get started!

- School trips
- Family vacations
- Picnics in the park
- Amusement park visits
- Days at the beach
- Birthday parties

Memorable Moments

Fill in your favorite memories in the spheres provided!

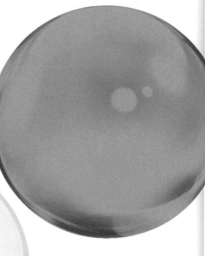

Imagination Land is a special place where all of Riley's creativity stems from. Using your imagination is important, because it helps you be creative! What kinds of things do you think would be in your Imagination Land?

THINGS IN MY IMAGINATION LAND

1. ....
....

2. ....
....

3. ....
....

4. ....
....

THINGS IN RILEY'S IMAGINATION LAND

- French Fry Forest
- Cloud Town
- Trophy Town
- House of Cards

Change

Riley was sad when her parents told her they were moving across the country. Dealing with change is never easy. But change is a big part of life, and it can be a great, big **WONDERFUL** opportunity!

What do you mean?

Look for the silver lining to any big change! Here are some examples.

MOVING

1. See more of the world.
2. Decorate a new room.
3. Join new clubs or activities.
4. Explore new neighborhoods.
5. Meet different people.

Change is so scary!

It doesn't have to be! What are some **BIG CHANGES** you are facing right now? How can you make the most of these changes?

CHANGE #1:  ....

1. ....
   ....
   ....

2. ....
   ....
   ....

3. ....
   ....
   ....

CHANGE #2: ....

1. ....
   ....
   ....

2. ....
   ....
   ....

3. ....
   ....
   ....

CHANGE #3: ....

1. ....
   ....
   ....

2. ....
   ....
   ....

3. ....
   ....
   ....

Character

It was hard for Riley to accept her new life in San Francisco. She tried to run away, but running from her problems only made them worse!

There will be times in your life when you can't control everything, but you can always control how you react.

If you are facing a difficult **DECISION**, ask yourself the following questions.

- What are my options?
- Who else will be affected by my decision?
- Will this decision get me into trouble?
- Is this the right thing to do, or just the easiest thing to do?
- Will this decision make me feel good about myself?
- Will it make my family proud of me?

School

One of the hardest parts about moving for Riley was going to a new school. It's overwhelming to meet so many new classmates and teachers and to remember all their names.

Even if you haven't moved, school can be tough! It's normal to be worried about homework, projects, and getting good grades. It helps to remember that everyone else is in the same boat!

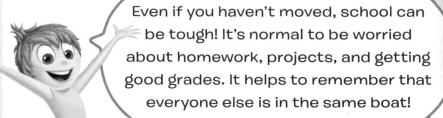

Below are some ways to make school a little easier!

TIPS AND TRICKS

- Show up early so you don't have to rush!

- Get a building map from the front office. Plan your route beforehand so you know exactly where to go!

- Come prepared with all your books and supplies. Color-code your books to make planning easier.

- Get to know your teachers. They'll appreciate the extra effort!

- Be friendly to everyone you meet. You never know who might become your new best friend!

Bullies, Cliques, and Getting Along

Riley could tell right away who the cool kids were in her new class. It's normal to want classmates to like you, but don't pretend to be someone you're not to impress others.

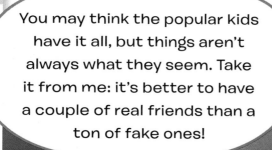

You may think the popular kids have it all, but things aren't always what they seem. Take it from me: it's better to have a couple of real friends than a ton of fake ones!

Disgust is right! Choosing people to be your friends is important. You may run into kids who act nice sometimes but at other times will ignore you or be rude.

I hate that!

Or you or one of your friends might become the target of a bully. If this happens, talk to a grown-up you trust, like a parent, teacher, or guidance counselor. They can give you advice on what to do. Remember: you're not alone!

QUIZ: ARE YOU IN THE RIGHT GROUP OF FRIENDS?

- Do your friends call and text you as much as you do them?

- Are they supportive of the things you do or want to do?

- Do your friends make you feel good about yourself?

- Are they nice to other kids, even ones they're not friends with?

- Do your friends respect your decisions and not pressure you to do things you aren't comfortable with?

If you answered "no" to any of these questions, you may want to branch out and make some new friends. It's good to have different groups of friends. That way, you always have options and a choice of multiple things to do!

Quiz: Are YOU a good friend?

- Do you act like you're better than other people?

- Have you ever not let a friend be "in the group"?

- Do you tease other people about their clothing or appearance?

- Have you ever told a friend you wouldn't like him or her unless they did what you want?

- Have you said things about your friends to make other kids laugh?

If you answered "yes" to any of these questions, you should think about why you acted this way and how you can be a better friend.

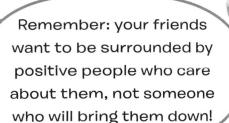

Remember: your friends want to be surrounded by positive people who care about them, not someone who will bring them down!

What did you say?

Oh, nothing . . .

Loneliness

Not knowing anyone in San Francisco was hard for Riley. She felt left out, like no one understood what she was going through.

Everyone feels lonely sometimes. But being lonely doesn't always mean you're alone. If you're missing a personal connection, it's possible to be lonely, even with other people around.

Here are a few ways to handle loneliness

- Reach out to someone you don't usually hang out with. It's possible this person could also use a new friend!

- Turn your loneliness into something positive—look for opportunities to volunteer or help someone who needs a hand!

- Use your time alone to start a new project or finish an old one.

- See the time by yourself as an opportunity for rest, relaxation, and daydreaming. Sit near a window and watch the world go by.

- Start a journal to get in touch with your thoughts, goals, and dreams!

Dreams

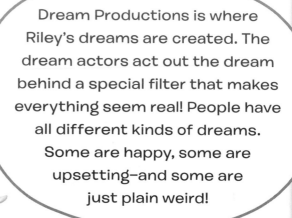

Dream Productions is where Riley's dreams are created. The dream actors act out the dream behind a special filter that makes everything seem real! People have all different kinds of dreams. Some are happy, some are upsetting—and some are just plain weird!

COMMON DREAMS

- Being chased
- Falling
- Eating dessert
- Being unable to speak
- Flying
- Forgetting about a test
- Teeth falling out
- Being late

Here are some of my dreams

....

....

....

....

....

....

....

....

....

....

....

....

Joy

Everyone's Emotions are different. Draw what you think the Five Emotions in your head would look like!

Sadness

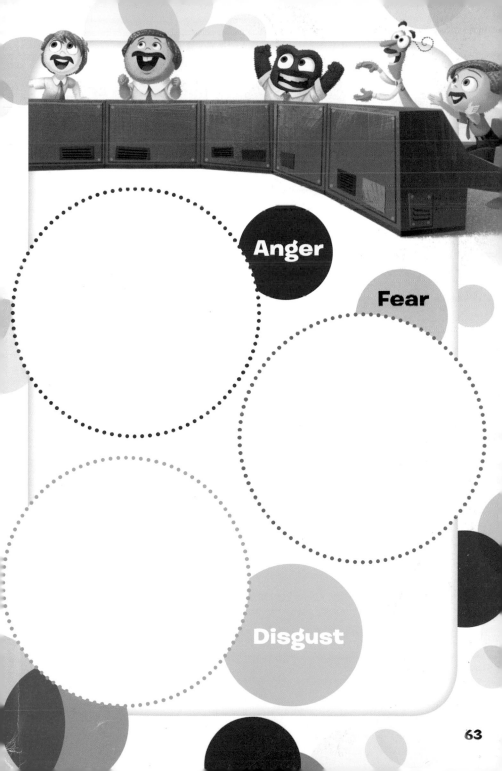

Anger

Fear

Disgust

CONCLUSION

Growing up brings with it a crazy mix of feelings!

Everyone has good days, bad days, and everything in between.

It's how we handle things that makes all the difference! By understanding and expressing our Emotions in a healthy way, we make better decisions and get along more easily with our friends and family.

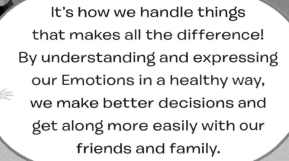

Signing off, this is **Joy**, **Sadness**, **Anger**, **Fear**, and **Disgust**.

Good luck!